GENERATIONAL GENEROSITY

GENERATIONAL GENEROSITY

Copyright © 2022, Nathan King & Richard Rogers

Published by NK Solutions, LLC.

All rights reserved. Printed in the United States of America. No part of this book may be used, reproduced in any manner, stored in a retrieval system, or transmitted in any form by any means—electronic, mechanical, photocopy, recording, or otherwise—without prior written permission of the author, except in the case of brief quotations embodied in critical articles and reviews, or as provided by United States of America copyright law.

Cover design by Nathan King

Edited by Pat Taylor

ISBN: 978-1-7374691-4-8

EBOOK ISBN: 978-1-7374691-5-5

Scripture quotations marked ESV are from the ESV® Bible (The Holy Bible, English Standard Version®), copyright © 2001 by Crossway Bibles, a publishing ministry of Good News Publishers. Used by permission. All rights reserved.

Scripture quotations labeled MSG are taken from THE MESSAGE. Copyright © 1993, 1994, 1995, 1996, 2000, 2001, 2002. Used by permission of NavPress Publishing Group.

Scripture quotations labeled NIV are from THE HOLY BIBLE, NEW INTERNATIONAL VERSION®, NIV® Copyright © 1973, 1978, 1984, 2011 by Biblica, Inc.™ Used by permission. All rights reserved worldwide.

For those discipling the next generation.

INTRODUCTION: PASSING THE BATON

One day an old farmer was splitting firewood in his front yard when a new truck came to a stop on the highway in front of his house. The farmer went to investigate. In his friendly way he called out to the stalled travelers. The three of them examined the truck and discovered a damaged tire. This was no good—not late on a Friday afternoon miles from the nearest tire shop. The travelers had been on their way to a local football game to watch their son compete. What were they to do? The older farmer did something few of us would think to do. He took out the keys to his old beat up pickup and handed them to the strangers.

I (Nathan) wasn't there to witness this uncommon act of generosity, but I've heard the story all of my life. My dad was right there watching as my grandfather handed a total stranger the keys to his only truck.

What compels people to such generosity? We all

recognize generous people when we see them at work. Their stories are the ones that breathe life into an all too often dismal news cycle. They are the ones who randomly buy a crowd of strangers their morning coffee. They are the ones who come through for a faltering non-profit when other resources have been exhausted. Generous people change the world every day while the rest of us stare in awe—and sometimes bewilderment.

The struggle to be generous (and it is very much a struggle) is first and foremost a matter of the heart. It's not about our wallet, our balance sheets, or any other measurable resource. Generosity is the willingness to give something within your power to give in the service of something beyond you.

Let me be blunt for a moment. God doesn't need you, He doesn't need me. And still God chooses to operate within our talents, time, and treasure to accomplish the work of *His* Kingdom. Why? Because of what it does in us and for us.

Living a generous life changes us. For the better. Forever.

For over a decade I (Richard) have asked questions about financial generosity to thousands of Christians in various leadership roles. The more conversations I have, the more I'm convinced we must be intentional if we are going to be effective in impacting this area of discipleship in the American church. Intentional discipleship starts with leading ourselves. We can't pass a baton we aren't carrying.

Whether your opportunity for growth is personal or you have a desire to impact leaders in your church, friends in your small group, or the kids in your home, being intentional is the key. We wrote this devotional to help you make an impact beyond yourself, beyond your church, even beyond your lifetime. You truly can influence generational generosity.

WEEK 1: STEWARDSHIP
"WHAT WE BELIEVE."

For the next three weeks we will focus on three areas that shape generosity. A friend and colleague, Joel Mikell, was the first person I remember clearly distinguishing between the meanings of Stewardship, Giving and Generosity.

Stewardship is *what we believe* about our relationship with money and possessions.

Giving is *what we do* in response to what we believe about our role as stewards.

Generosity is part of our identity developed through faithful giving. It's a reflection of our character. It is *who we become*.

Stewardship... the truth is most of us don't spend a lot of time thinking about what we believe. We might share our opinion about how we prioritize our resources, why we give to the church, or how we feel about debt. But have we spent time building a foundation in regard to these issues, based on aligning our heart with God's heart, for the purpose of living into those beliefs for the benefit of others?

DAY 1
IT ALL BELONGS TO GOD

The earth is the Lord's, and everything in it, the world, and all who live in it... (Psalm 24:1 NIV)

Breathtaking. That's the immediate word that comes to mind when I try to describe the places in which I often find myself. I'm an avid outdoorsman. So I seem to routinely find myself cresting some peak, or rounding a bend on the side of a mountain that leaves me staring into the wide open expanse in wonder. We live in a beautiful world. My family has made it one of our joyous pursuits to see a lot of it—and it is breathtaking.

The beauty of this world is something to marvel at. And, it was made for you. God did it. But it doesn't belong to you. Every time I make the peak and stare off across an emerald ocean of sun kissed evergreens I'm looking out on a landscape that doesn't belong to me. I'm catching a moment of serenity given to me by God, but the vista is God's. At best we're managers. We are stewards. God has chosen to give me this moment in time to enjoy it.

Many years ago stewards were common. A steward was the most trusted and capable servant of the household. He was trusted to administrate and care for everything the owner had. Stewards are not very common anymore. It's important for us to understand because it's who we are. We are stewards. We have been entrusted with this world and all its resources by a really good God.

God chose to make you a manager of what is not yours. In all of the cosmos—including this earth—teaming with life and resources was entrusted to you. God trusts you with His world. Amazing.

Our responsibility is to become the best steward we can be. Growing and learning in the values that will empower us to become the diligent stewards God wants us to be. God trusts you. Think about that the next time you catch a crimson sunset as it settles on the horizon. Let it compel you to become the best steward possible.

FOR REFLECTION OR DISCUSSION:

Why is it difficult in our culture to see ourselves as merely stewards instead of owners?

_____
_____
_____
_____
_____
_____
_____
_____

Is it harder for you to faithfully manage time, talent or treasure?

_____
_____
_____
_____
_____
_____
_____
_____

CHALLENGE:

Make a note of something you steward well.

_____
_____
_____
_____
_____
_____
_____
_____

DAY 2
STRONG BEGINNINGS

Start children off on the way they should go, and even when they are old they will not turn from it. (Proverbs 22:6 NIV)

One night after dinner my dad handed me a map and said, "I need you to calculate the direction for this fence." My dad, ever the school teacher, knew that at the time I was studying trigonometry in high school. Mrs. Smith, my teacher, was both his colleague and a family friend. She knew I was struggling a bit. (I'm convinced they had concocted this plan together.) I sat for hours working at the problem—until finally I arrived at a solution.

The importance of those first few feet were pretty significant. Just a degree or two off in the beginning would account for a significant issue at the end. The final part of the fence would have been way off. So my dad wanted it to start off going in the right direction. But it wasn't all about the fence. My dad also wanted me to develop a skill he knew could be useful later. He cared about showing me the way my life should go too.

I've never used that particular set of trig skills again: Sorry, Mrs. Smith! But I did come to appreciate the significance of going in the right direction. As a father, pastor, and teacher—I am continually thinking about how to help the important people in my life determine the way they should go.

In my family this means frequent conversations with my kids. If we're watching a movie and something interesting happens, we often pause the movie to discuss the situation and the decisions that are being made. We'll talk through the consequences and what might have been different. Why? I want my kids to understand the importance of the way they should go.

FOR REFLECTION OR DISCUSSION:

What are some areas in life where it's important to get off to a good start?

_____
_____
_____
_____
_____
_____

Did you have someone who mentored or supported you in something to help you succeed or accomplish a goal?

_____
_____
_____
_____
_____

CHALLENGE:

Take 10-15 minutes to handwrite a brief "Thank you" note to someone who has helped you with a strong beginning. And **SEND IT TO THEM!** Write their name below.

_____

DAY 3
BEING INTENTIONAL

Love the Lord your God with all your heart and with all your soul and with all your strength. These commandments that I give you today are to be on your hearts. Impress them on your children. Talk about them when you sit at home and when you walk along the road, when you lie down and when you get up. (Deuteronomy 6:5-7 NIV)

The bowls clanged, dinnerware clinked, and the murmur of chewing and eating settled on our dining room. It's a scene we repeat most nights of the week—dinner time. The food is always changing, but the cast is the same. My wife Jamie, myself, and our four kids settle into whatever is on the nightly menu while our dog Joy tries to snipe crumbs from beneath the kids' places around the table.

Usually this is the part of our day when we share stories, talk about what transpired at work and school, and think of fun things to do together. Occasionally the talk will take a turn toward something we like to call a teachable moment. My wife is quick to both see it and seize it. She's spent a long time working with young kids in a variety of contexts and is so good at pointing out a life lesson from an argument about green beans while I'm still busy cutting up my pork chop.

You and I are given opportunities everyday to be intentional—with the ones we love, and with total strangers too. Generosity begins by taking advantage of those opportunities.

At home it means intentionally realizing the kids I'm raising are tomorrow's leaders. I need to lean into each opportunity to pass along valuable lessons in order to wisely manage the skill set they will need to possess so they in turn can manage resources for future generations.

FOR REFLECTION OR DISCUSSION:

Can you name someone who has been intentional about investing in your life?

_____
_____
_____
_____
_____

How has that made an impact on you?

_____
_____
_____
_____
_____

CHALLENGE:

Write down the name of someone God has placed in this season of your life that you can impact.

_____
_____

DAY 4
THE GIFT

Don't you see that children are God's best gift? The fruit of the womb his generous legacy? (Psalm 127:3 MSG)

Do you remember what it was like when your kids were little? Or, perhaps you've watched friends walk this out. They show up to everything exhausted. There is a nearly universal look to parents with young kids. They are tired.

I've lived in some kind of state of child-induced-tiredness for a decade. Late nights rocking them back to sleep, surprise diapers in the middle of my rem cycle. Early mornings stifling tears—way before the alarm I had set the night before. It's a pretty normal part of parenting. But we do it. Even when it hurts, which is a lot of time when our kids are young.

Parents do all kinds of things for their children. Why? Because we innately understand the genuine gift from God that kids really are.

Your kids are a gift from God. That's so important I'm going to say it again. Your kids are a gift from God. You've been blessed with the sacred privilege of stewarding the life of a human being. What could be more amazing? Nothing—so let's get it right.

If your parenting journey has been anything like mine you're frequently tired, that means you are doing a great job. You are consistently giving your energy and effort to care for their well-being. You are being generous with your life in order to best care for the life of another.

Parenting is a pretty great reminder of the generous life God wants for all of us. Yes, God trusts us to steward this world. But for those of us called mom or dad, God also entrusts us with something much more important—the gift of stewarding another life.

FOR REFLECTION OR DISCUSSION:

What is a recent gift you've received?

_____
_____
_____

How did you respond?

_____
_____
_____

If you are a parent, what is one hope you have for your child(ren)?

_____
_____
_____
_____

What is something you are modeling that you believe will bless them once they are old enough to appreciate it?

_____
_____
_____
_____
_____

CHALLENGE:

Write the names of your children below. Thank God for each one by name. Call them this week and tell them you are thankful for them.

_____
_____
_____
_____
_____
_____
_____
_____
_____
_____

DAY 5
TRUST

Trust God from the bottom of your heart; don't try to figure out everything on your own. Listen for God's voice in everything you do, everywhere you go; he's the one who will keep you on track. (Proverbs 3:5-6 MSG)

Years ago, before kids, I was an avid rock climber. I loved scaling the face of some big cliff and then experiencing the joy of rappelling back down. The rapid descent was an exultant reward for the challenging ascent to the top.

Trust is a huge part of the climbing sport. You have to trust your equipment. You have to trust your partner. You have to trust that rock sticking out you're about to bet your weight on.

God is truly hoping you will trust him like that. He really wants us to know we don't have to do it all on our own. Yes, God trusts us to manage this world. God trusts us to raise our families. But God also wants us to come to him for help.

Real trust is more than a surface issue. We all know people who say they trust someone but maybe when that person isn't around their actions make it clear that they don't *really* trust them.

We need to trust God beyond the surface, like you are hanging on to Him for dear life. Trust God loves you more than you can imagine. Trust God has forgiven your past. Trust God has your best interest at heart. A big part of trusting God includes recognizing what God has entrusted to you. Your family for starters. But also the other relationships in your life. Find out what will move you away from doubt and toward trust.

FOR REFLECTION OR DISCUSSION:

What is something that you trust easily each day?

_____
_____
_____
_____
_____

Why is it easier to trust your own efforts than to rely upon God?

_____
_____
_____
_____
_____

CHALLENGE:

Share with your spouse or a friend your thoughts about this statement: "The way we use our resources reflects our trust in God's ability to provide for us."

_____
_____
_____
_____
_____

DAY 6
LEAST BIT

Speaking to the people, he went on, "Take care! Protect yourself against the least bit of greed. Life is not defined by what you have, even when you have a lot." (Luke 12:15 MSG)

The last time my family went to the beach we had two kids. Our parenting duties have doubled since then and we're long overdue for another swing at some fun in the sandy sun. Sign me up. But there's one part of the beach I'm not crazy about–the sand. I know. I know. You're thinking, *"Nate the beach is literally sand."* You're not wrong.

I love the beautiful greens and blues of the ocean as

it catches the sun. My favorite part is the rolling waves and playing in the water. But my least favorite part is the sand that gets everywhere. It gets in and on everything. It drives me nuts.

Greed and sand aren't so different. Greed gets everywhere. And once you're playing around with it it's hard to get away from. It clings to you. Often in surprising ways.

The answer to greed is a lot like the answer to sand. At the end of every day at the beach my wife and I take the time to wash the sand off of things. We go through toys and bags and make sure to pour any sand out. We don't want even a grain left. Why? Because even a grain of sand can cause problems.

Wash yourself of greed. How? By being generous. It's hard to be greedy with open hands. Examine the parts of your heart and your life where being generous seems the most challenging. If you are prone to being greedy with your time—scrutinize your daily routines and schedule. If financial resources (aka money) are where you're greedy, ask yourself why. Figure it out.

Another great way to overcome greed in your life is by remembering you're a steward. Remember, we are responsible for getting the resources under our care to those most in need of them. Don't let what you hold on to define you. Be known for what you let go of.

FOR REFLECTION OR DISCUSSION:

What is a little thing that can become a big thing if left unchecked?

_____
_____
_____

What do you tend to guard more closely - your time, your talents, or your money?

_____
_____
_____

How do you discern the difference between being cautious and being greedy?

_____
_____
_____

CHALLENGE:

Say a brief prayer asking God if there is sand clinging to you that needs to be washed off. Invite God to turn on the water.

DAY 7
IMMEASURABLY MORE

Now to him who is able to do immeasurably more than all we ask or imagine, according to his power that is at work within us, to him be glory in the church and in Christ Jesus throughout all generations, for ever and ever! Amen. (Ephesians 3:20-21 NIV)

One winter my dad gave me a task to complete as we worked on a new fence. I was in charge of unrolling an extremely long stretch of barbed wire through a forest for almost half a mile. I was cold, the task seemed to be taking forever, and I couldn't even begin to understand why it was important. I was frustrated. Just as I grew fed up with trying to complete my chore I looked up and saw where I was. I was at the end. My dad reminded me that every fence begins with the first wire. He wanted me to learn the importance of every step and every wire.

As a twelve year old boy I couldn't contemplate the significance of that first step through the woods. I didn't understand the bigger picture behind each inch gained in my task. And because I was in the middle of a forest I didn't see the grand design for what was going on. I couldn't see how my father was at work just ahead of me.

As those who trust God it's our job to make our next move in faith. We each are stewards of the steps we take each day. All you can do is be faithful to your next step. The beauty of every step is that your Father is at work just ahead of you.

There is always a bigger picture, more going on than you can imagine, because God is up to something. You have been called into a plan larger than you can imagine. Your significance will sometimes seem a mystery; but it's all part of God's plan.

Take your faithful next step. Trust that God is doing more than you can imagine, more than you can measure, and more than you can see. God is asking us to step up to what He's busy setting up. As we trust

God for our next step He is trusting us too. What's God trusting us with? Immeasurably more than we can imagine.

FOR REFLECTION OR DISCUSSION:

Are you a big picture person, or do you tend to focus more on the moment?

_____
_____
_____
_____
_____

What are the advantages to each perspective?

_____
_____
_____
_____
_____

CHALLENGE:

Write down a "next step" in a significant area that you need to take.

_____
_____
_____
_____
_____

WEEK 2: GIVING
"WHAT WE DO."

Giving... stewardship isn't enough. Knowledge doesn't become wisdom until it's acted upon. Understanding stewardship from a Christian perspective is like having knowledge - it's a great place to start. If you want to move from knowledge to wisdom you must take action. If you want to move from stewardship toward generosity then you must take action, and that action must align behavior with beliefs. The reality is that our actions do indeed reflect our beliefs which is why it's so important to first think deeply about stewardship, make conscious decisions about aligning our lives with the heart of God, and then taking action. How will you respond?

DAY 8
GOD GAVE

For God so loved the world that he gave his one and only Son, that whoever believes in him shall not perish but have eternal life. (John 3:16 NIV)

On a beautiful Sunday afternoon my friend Ron walked out of church service with his family. As they made their way across the parking lot something caught Ron's attention. It was a truck flying down the street directly in front of the church. The truck was headed right for a small kid crossing the road. Ron simply reacted. He stepped into the street, scooped up the kid tossing him to safety just as the speeding vehicle crashed into him. Ron suffered an incredible impact that shattered his leg and traumatized his body.

Twenty years later Ron walks with a limp. Extreme generosity left its mark on his life—literally. If I know my friend, he would do it again in a heartbeat. Why? Because he is the kind of guy willing to give it all to help someone in need.

We have an example in giving that we can never live up to. The beautiful thing about it is that we aren't expected to. God gave His Son Jesus in order to atone for the sins of the world. In order to atone for our sins. God set the example for radical generosity. Nothing is more generous than giving away life itself.

You and I will likely never be asked to give away our very lives. Likely, we may never even come as close as my friend Ron. But we can be ready to be generous. And once our heart for generosity has become more like Christ's—like Ron—it will be something we don't even have to think about. We just act because it's who we are.

FOR REFLECTION OR DISCUSSION:

Has the act of giving become easy for you yet, or do you still have to make a conscious decision before giving something away?

_____
_____
_____
_____
_____

What is one way you can be *ready* to give, so that you are *able* to give when the opportunity arises?

_____
_____
_____
_____
_____

CHALLENGE:

Consider tucking an appropriate amount of cash away in your purse or wallet for the express purpose of giving it away when you are prompted to give it.

DAY 9
RETURNING

What shall I return to the Lord for all his goodness to me? (Psalm 116:12 NIV)

Each day I try to make talking about God's goodness a conscious action. Why? Because God has been so good to me. All the good things in my life have their roots in and can be traced back to the incredible ways God has helped me. The end result has me continually wondering how I can give back.

The truth is it all belongs to God already. The way He trusts me with it is humbling, inspiring, and sometimes intimidating. Because I know I'm not giving it back to God out of compulsion or out of the desire to pay some kind of debt (that's not how grace works) I, instead, find myself looking for what I can give that will be the most beneficial to my everyday world.

I give financially to my church. My wife and I do that faithfully at the beginning of each month. But we don't stop there. Long before I was on a church payroll we were giving our time and talents to the church as well. That's part of returning to God what He has given to me. God gave me the talents I have that can benefit the body of Christ. God gave me the breath in my lungs that allows me to live each day in search of another opportunity to help someone.

Not everything I give relates to the local gathering place we call our church either. We should also be looking for ways that we can add value to the kingdom of God right where we are. You can return value to the kingdom from your cubicle. You can make a difference in eternity with a conversation in the grocery store aisle. Consider how God has been good to you, and look for ways to return God's goodness in kind.

FOR REFLECTION OR DISCUSSION:

What role does gratitude play in our motivations to give?

_____
_____
_____
_____
_____

What do you think about the idea of "returning" versus "giving" in this context?

_____
_____
_____
_____
_____

CHALLENGE:

Find a way to "return God's goodness" to someone today. Be intentional about being a blessing to someone in a practical way for them.

DAY 10
BRINGING

Bring the whole tithe into the storehouse, that there may be food in my house. Test me in this," says the Lord Almighty, "and see if I will not throw open the floodgates of heaven and pour out so much blessing that there will not be room enough to store it. (Malachi 3:10 NIV)

There's a piece of me that cringes a little bit anytime I hear someone say they need to "pay their tithes". Because tithing is not like your electric bill or your insurance premiums. The church doesn't bill you for services rendered.

The tithe is something we bring. Remember, it's already God's. He has only entrusted you with it. You and I are stewards of our resources. When we tithe, we bring 10% of what God has enabled us to earn back to the church so it can be used strategically to advance the gospel. In giving the first tenth we acknowledge we are stewards. It forces our focus outward.

If I bring my tithe, Richard brings his, and Mark brings his, there will be more available for the kingdom of God to put to use than if each of us simply tried to do it on our own. The act of bringing the tithe allows us to participate in the growth of an eternal kingdom.

The blessing that follows our obedience can't be measured and isn't even always known to us. When our heart is properly aligned with the vision and mission of the church to reach people with the love of Christ we will receive an internal reward for participating in that mission. It's something that is hard to articulate, but there is a sense of joy and fulfillment in coming together as a church financially and making a significant impact in the community, the city, and the world in which we live.

FOR REFLECTION OR DISCUSSION:

Where did you learn about tithing?

_____
_____
_____
_____
_____

Have you made it a priority to "bring the whole tithe into the storehouse?"

_____
_____
_____
_____
_____

CHALLENGE:

Ask a friend in your life group or Sunday School class about why they give to the church. Write their response.

_____
_____
_____
_____
_____

DAY 11
HEART'S DESIRE

Don't hoard treasure down here where it gets eaten by moths and corroded by rust or—worse! —stolen by burglars. Stockpile treasure in heaven, where it's safe from moth and rust and burglars. It's obvious, isn't it? The place where your treasure is, is the place you will most want to be, and end up being. (Matthew 6:19-21 MSG)

Several years ago my wife and I made a significant turn around in our financial situation. Up until that moment we had struggled with debt and living paycheck to paycheck. But it changed when a mentor challenged us to look at our expenses as a reflection of our heart. I took him up on the challenge and quickly realized my money situation was out of control because my heart was out of control. I was spending selfishly—often. I learned that you will put your money where you put your heart.

While I certainly still believe in that principle I think there is one that is even more powerful we can internalize. Yes, your bank statement reflects your heart in many ways. But, have you ever considered how your calendar reflects your heart? As enlightening as it was to examine my bank statement for a heart condition—my calendar was so much more revealing.

If I say my family is the most important thing in my life but routinely work 85 hours a week—I'm deceiving myself. I'm not trying to be mean. I am trying to be helpful. Where our heart is—that is where we will be. Our presence reveals our desire.

My friend Josh is an incredible example of this. He walked away from an incredibly lucrative career. He took a massive decrease in pay at a much more physically demanding job. Why? Because he wanted to spend more time with his family.

God's desire for each of us is not to hoard what we have here, but to treasure who we have. God wants us to use our resources (time, talent, and treasure) in a way that reflects our love for Him and for one another. The way we do it will reveal the sincerity of our commitment.

FOR REFLECTION OR DISCUSSION:

What are 3 or 4 things that are most important to you?

_____
_____
_____
_____

CHALLENGE:

Jot down in 5-7 categories how you typically spend the 168 hours in a week. Some possible categories might be sleeping, working, eating, playing, exercising, relaxing, learning, thinking, planning, serving, praying, worshiping. Roughly allocate hours to the categories you chose. Is there anything noteworthy in what you see?

_____
_____
_____
_____
_____
_____
_____
_____
_____

DAY 12
GIVE IT AWAY

Give away your life; you'll find life given back, but not merely given back—given back with bonus and blessing. Giving, not getting, is the way. Generosity begets generosity. (Luke 6:38 MSG)

Every good thing that has happened to me in my adult life has been the result of selflessness. What's really wild about that idea to me is the reality that I have still spent so much time and energy being selfish. Maybe it's a guy thing, or a result of my driven personality—but I truly have mustered a lot of effort in service to myself.

Still, when I take a look back at the trajectory of my relationships, my career, and my opportunities I realized all of the most significant things have happened as a result of giving. I met my wife when I decided to give a year of my life to serving college students at a local university. I became a pastor at a really healthy church when I left a nice full time ministry position to become a volunteer. Doors opened for my family when we made it our mission to give of ourselves.

It's almost paradoxical the way it works. How could we give something away and then all of a sudden see it create more than we started with? Simple. That's just how God works. In the kingdom of God one plus one doesn't always equal two. Sometimes it equals twenty.

The path to the best life is the one in which you hold things loosely. Not because you're flippant or irresponsible—but because you are laser focused on adding value around you. Generosity opens doors you will never see coming.

FOR REFLECTION OR DISCUSSION:

What is your first reaction when you think about giving something away?

_____
_____
_____
_____
_____

Have you experienced a time when you sacrificed something and then were surprised by God's provision?

_____
_____
_____
_____
_____
_____

CHALLENGE:

Remove a time waster from your life and make an intentional choice to add value to others around you. Delete that app or watch one less episode and commit one hour this week to making a difference for someone else.

DAY 13
EXCELLING

But since you excel in everything—in faith, in speech, in knowledge, in complete earnestness and in the love we have kindled in you—see that you also excel in this grace of giving. (2 Corinthians 8:7 NIV)

I'm not wired for mediocrity. I just can't do it. Blame it on my dad, but I can't settle for doing something only halfway. If I'm going to take on a task I want to go at it with everything I've got. I want it to be excellent. In fact, in our church we believe, "Excellence honors God and inspires people."

It's no small thing to excel in the grace of giving. It

may seem like the grace of giving is in rare supply, but I actually firmly believe it's overshadowed by a selfish and proud culture. There are many incredible people out there who are giving graciously everyday. They teach our kids, serve our communities, and protect our streets.

I think you are like one of those. Even if you haven't started yet. I believe you are the kind of person God has been waiting to pick up the slack in your everyday world. What if someone you run into on a regular basis has been waiting for you? What kind of difference will you make in your neighborhood, church, or business by becoming someone known for excelling in the grace of giving?

Everything about the story of the gospel is marked by the extravagance of giving what is undeserved to those who can never earn it. As we learn to become more like Christ we will also learn to strive to exhibit the grace of giving.

When the grace of giving marks our lives in excess people will hear it in the words we say. They will feel it in our embrace. They will know it in the way we change the room when we walk in. Because of the excellent gift of grace operating in your life things will get better around you.

FOR REFLECTION OR DISCUSSION:

What is an area of your life where those who know you best would say that you excel?

_____
_____
_____
_____
_____

Why do you think the Apostle Paul referred to it as "...this *grace* of giving?"

_____
_____
_____
_____
_____

CHALLENGE:

If you haven't already done so, commit to giving a specific percentage of your income away for the next 30 days. If you are already a percentage giver, increase the percentage you give away by 1-2% of your income for the next 30 days.

DAY 14
DELIGHTING

Remember: A stingy planter gets a stingy crop; a lavish planter gets a lavish crop. I want each of you to take plenty of time to think it over, and make up your own mind what you will give. That will protect you against sob stories and arm-twisting. God loves it when the giver delights in the giving. (2 Corinthians 9:6-7 MSG)

This is probably going to sound creepy, but sometimes I like to just stand back and watch my kids interacting with each other—especially if I can do it when they have no idea I am there. Why? Because there is an honesty to it. They are behaving independent of my direct influence.

Sometimes I see them struggle with one another or fight over a toy. Those moments are real. But so are the moments when I watch them share. When my four-year-old hands my two-year-old a toy and speaks to her in his sweet voice I see it for what it is—sincere giving.

If you're a parent, what I'm about to say won't surprise you. They don't always share. They don't always show one another grace. And neither do we. Rarely is the first thing on our mind *"How can I give something to the person right across from me?"* That's not how our mind works. Not for most of us.

Generosity is a near constant struggle for human culture. Some people are predisposed to be extremely generous. Some are hardwired to hoard everything they can. And there's a sizable chunk that lives between the extremes.

Giving is always more fun when it is our own idea. There is an honesty and purity to it. In those moments when God has helped me operate in generosity it does something amazing. It lifts me up. I become cheerful at the prospect of giving.

God invites each of us to live so that giving is a cheerful act. We give, not because we have been manipulated, but because we want to see how it will help someone else.

FOR REFLECTION OR DISCUSSION:

When have you experienced joy or delight from giving to someone else?

_____
_____
_____
_____
_____

Describe the situation and how it made you feel.

_____
_____
_____
_____
_____
_____

CHALLENGE:

Give a ridiculously generous tip to a server in a restaurant this week.

WEEK 3: GENEROSITY
"WHO WE BECOME."

Generosity... what do those who know us best think about the life we are living? Not just what they will say at our funeral, but what about now? Generosity may be hard to define but we know it when we see it. When we think of a life characterized by generosity, it's typically one that's been built over time. So if you have a heart for generosity, a desire to reflect Christ, it's a great time to start practicing what you want to become until it is who you are.

DAY 15
BLESSED

Whoever has a bountiful eye will be blessed, for he shares his bread with the poor. (Proverbs 22:9 ESV)

There are people in this world who just see things differently than the rest of us. They look at a situation and innately understand the opportunity waiting on the other side. My friend Heath is wired this way. People like Heath get caught up in a way of life that seems to turn everything they touch into success. The beauty of this is that they don't hoard it to themselves like a mythical dragon on a pile of treasure. Instead, they bring everyone close to them along for the journey.

Generosity has always been a heart issue first and foremost. In order to let go of my time, talent, or treasure I have to be open to what it will do for the one I am giving it to. I have to see the potential in what's about to happen. I don't know about you, but that's not always easy.

Just like everything else about generosity, the ones who have become wildly generous in their approach to life know that in the end it actually blesses them. It seems like nonsense. How can my life get better if I give everything away? How can I be more fulfilled? How could I actually wind up with even more? In what economy does that make sense? In God's economy.

The problem too many of us bring to the table when it comes to generosity is that we know how to do math. Because absolutely $1 - 1 = 0$. My math teaching wife would be proud. Except that's not exactly how it works with God.

If I had something and gave it to someone else I didn't lose it. They gained it. And I learned the beauty and power of what it could mean for them and the potential for doing it. I've seen again and again how God will take someone like that and show them the opportunity to give it again, and again, and again.

FOR REFLECTION OR DISCUSSION:

How does our inclination to share resources with others reflect our view of the scarcity or abundance of those resources?

_____
_____
_____
_____
_____
_____
_____

Can you remember a time when you did not have enough of something and it led to an insecurity you still carry?

_____
_____
_____
_____
_____
_____
_____
_____

CHALLENGE:

Talk to a trusted friend or family member about God's blessing in your life. What are the obvious signs of God providing you ways to be a blessing to someone else?

_____
_____
_____
_____
_____
_____
_____
_____
_____
_____
_____

DAY 16
REPUTATION

Sunrise breaks through the darkness for good people— God's grace and mercy and justice! The good person is generous and lends lavishly; No shuffling or stumbling around for this one, But a sterling and solid and lasting reputation. (Psalm 112:4-6 MSG)

How do people feel about you when you're not around? That's your reputation. Do they get mad when they think about what you did in the office? Are they sad because you're no longer part of their everyday circle? The memory you leave behind says a lot about the way you conduct your life.

Generous people leave a trail of devastating kindness and hope. Their reputation is not hard to look back on. You can see where they've been because of how much they changed things.

The most significant moments in my life are tied up with people I encountered who lavishly and extravagantly poured into me. They gave me hope. They gave me kindness when I needed it. They gave me mentoring when there was nothing in it for them. They left a trail in my life of many good things.

I hope one day people will say, "Nate was faithful." That's the reputation I want. I want to be faithful to my wife, my family, my church, and my opportunities. But I can't be faithful if I hold back. Instead, I want to lean in. I'm convinced you do too.

Let's aim our life at the kind of living that isn't leaving broken relationships in our rear view mirror. Instead, let's treat every day like a memory we want someone to hold on to of us forever.

FOR REFLECTION OR DISCUSSION:

Who is someone that immediately comes to mind when you think of generous people?

_____
_____
_____
_____
_____
_____
_____
_____

Why did their name surface in your thoughts?

_____
_____
_____
_____
_____
_____
_____

CHALLENGE:

Take 10-15 minutes to write a few sentences about the person you aspire to become. How do you want to be remembered? Start with a few key words that come to mind and then craft a sentence for each.

_____
_____
_____
_____
_____
_____
_____
_____
_____
_____
_____
_____
_____
_____

DAY 17
EXPANDING

The world of the generous gets larger and larger; the world of the stingy gets smaller and smaller. (Proverbs 11:24 MSG)

For years my friend Jake tried to get me to go with him to help some friends in Ecuador with a project. I kept telling him, "Thanks, but no thanks." But even back then I was trying to figure out how to be a generous guy so God kept working on my heart. One day Jake asked again. I don't know who was more surprised, me or Jake, when I replied, "Okay, I will go."

Up until then I'd never flown before. I'd never really left my small little part of the world. I'll never forget my first look out the window of that giant jet as we rocketed through the sky. In one afternoon my worldview changed forever.

It doesn't take a jaunt across the globe to shift your perspective. It takes being willing to participate in the generous action available to you right now, wherever you are. You don't have to board a jet with a suitcase and some headphones. You can just walk down the block with a box of donuts and a cell phone. Give the donuts away to people you see on your way to work. Call a friend and tell them how much they mean to you.

Generosity happens on purpose. So, do it on purpose. What you will find is that looking for opportunities to be generous will cause you to find them. As you do, the size of your world will shift. Why? Because generosity is uncontainable. Your heart grows in tandem with your horizons when you aim at living the kind of life that leaves a generous trail.

FOR REFLECTION OR DISCUSSION:

As you reread the Message translation of Proverbs 11:24, what do you think about the phrases contrasting the generous and the stingy?

_____
_____
_____
_____
_____
_____
_____
_____

Do you view your ability to impact others as expanding or contracting? Why?

_____
_____
_____
_____
_____
_____
_____
_____

CHALLENGE:

Do something on purpose today to expand your worldview and jot a few notes about that experience.

_____
_____
_____
_____
_____
_____
_____
_____
_____
_____
_____
_____
_____
_____

DAY 18
REFRESHING

A generous person will prosper; whoever refreshes others will be refreshed. (Proverbs 11:25 NIV)

Every couple of days my phone buzzes with an early morning text from my friend Jon. He's a generous guy in many ways, and his texts are always the same. He sends me one bible verse.

What I've learned to love about Jon's texts is the heart behind them. They are always encouraging texts that give me another arrow in my quiver of encouragement for the day. They are always refreshing. But Jon is being refreshed too.

Jon knows what all generous people know. Living a life of generosity is refreshing for those on the receiving end, but it's just as—if not more—refreshing for those doing the giving.

What does that even mean? Well, fresh means new. You think about fresh baked bread, fresh vegetables recently harvested, or even a brand new baby. We are drawn toward new things. There is so much potential in something new. When we are refreshed we are in the process of being new again.

Generosity changes your potential. It's not a new coat of paint on the old model. Being generous changes your heart over and over and over again. You become someone with a new lens each and every time you participate in genuine generosity. You aren't just giving stuff away—you are growing potential.

FOR REFLECTION OR DISCUSSION:

How is encouragement connected to generosity?

_____
_____
_____
_____

Think of a specific time recently when you have been refreshed or encouraged. Who was involved? How did you feel at that moment?

_____
_____
_____
_____
_____
_____
_____
_____
_____

CHALLENGE:

Place three coins in one front pocket or three small rings on one finger. Each time you encourage someone today, move one of the coins to another pocket, or one of the rings to another finger.

DAY 19
EVERYTHING

But a poor widow came and put in two very small copper coins, worth only a few cents. Calling his disciples to him, Jesus said, "Truly I tell you, this poor widow has put more into the treasury than all the others. They all gave out of their wealth; but she, out of her poverty, put in everything—all she had to live on." (Mark 12:42-44 NIV)

In the last two weeks I've learned more about floors than I ever really wanted to know. This came about because we decided to remodel our house. One day after work we started ripping up all of the old flooring.

In every room in our house I have found penny after penny under the old floors. Without thinking much about them I sat them aside—until one day my daughter found, not just one, but two pennies on the floor. She was ecstatic, exclaiming, "I found moneys!" Something I easily took for granted was a discovered treasure in the eyes of my child. She really challenged my thinking.

Jesus was always looking for an opportunity to challenge the thinking of His friends. It was certainly the case in the example of the widow with two pennies. Giving had become a point of pride among some of their contemporaries. So Jesus wanted to bring some correction to their way of thinking.

The amazing example laid down by the widow is one that astonishes us. It's challenging. She didn't stop at a fixed percentage when it came to giving. The widow made everything she had available to God. Throughout history, her trust, her commitment, and her sacrifice has been viewed as the ultimate example of generosity.

How we treat our approach to giving is a big indicator of where our heart is. If we treat the interaction like paying our taxes we're missing the mark. If we limit ourselves to a percentage point and never consider what God may be calling us to do, we may miss an opportunity for deeper trust or a blessing God wants us to experience.

FOR REFLECTION OR DISCUSSION:

What do you think the widow was thinking when she made her gift?

_____
_____
_____
_____
_____
_____
_____
_____

Have you seen anything that approaches this level of generosity modeled by someone? Do you know the story behind that gift?

_____
_____
_____
_____
_____
_____
_____

CHALLENGE:

Write down an area of your life where it has been easier for you to make your time, talents or treasure more available for God to use.

_____
_____
_____
_____
_____

Write down an area where it has been more difficult.

_____
_____
_____
_____
_____
_____

DAY 20
FINISHING WELL

What matters most to me is to finish what God started: the job the Master Jesus gave me of letting everyone I meet know all about this incredibly extravagant generosity of God. (Acts 20:24 MSG)

Several years ago I had the privilege of leading my church through an extensive renovation project. Up until that moment we had been holding Sunday services in a community building. Every Sunday morning we would come together and unload two semi truck trailers to build a welcoming space for our new congregation on a basketball court. We'd use a nearby hallway and auxiliary rooms for our kids spaces.

For an entire summer I spent nearly every day leading volunteers through the construction project. We knocked down walls, removed old HVAC units, we scraped, nailed, rolled, hammered, and painted for weeks—until finally the project was finished. As we neared completion everyone could feel the excitement building. It would have been easy to rush through the final touches. Only a handful of things were keeping us from being ready to move in. Two words become our guiding mantra, "Finish well." We knew that the finishing touches were going to be the things that stuck out when people first walked in. So we poured our love into every brushstroke. Why? Because each moment was an opportunity to show our new friends how much God loved them.

God's love for you and me is too big for us to really wrap our heads or our hearts around. It's pretty incredible. Generosity starts with God. God is the standard. Each thing we attempt in His name we should walk into with an incredible willingness to perform well. We want to start well—certainly, but never forget, how you finish is often what people remember. Let's live, and finish, like we're participating in the incredibly generous story God is shaping in the hearts of the people He loves.

FOR REFLECTION OR DISCUSSION:

Would you rather start something or finish something?

_____
_____
_____
_____
_____
_____
_____
_____

What would it look like for you to "finish what God started" in the area of financial generosity?

_____
_____
_____
_____
_____
_____
_____
_____

CHALLENGE:

Write down 3-5 names of people to whom you could provide leadership and encouragement in their generosity journey.

_____
_____
_____
_____
_____

Is there an appropriate next step you can take with any of the people you listed?

_____
_____
_____
_____
_____
_____
_____
_____
_____

DAY 21
TRULY LIFE

Tell those rich in this world's wealth to quit being so full of themselves and so obsessed with money, which is here today and gone tomorrow. Tell them to go after God, who piles on all the riches we could ever manage—to do good, to be rich in helping others, to be extravagantly generous. If they do that, they'll build a treasury that will last, gaining life that is truly life. (1 Timothy 6:17-19 MSG)

Jamie and I recently became pastors at a new church. On one hand it was a tough decision to make. On the other hand it wasn't so hard. Why? Because we believe in being generous and we saw the opportunity to give to more people the gifts God has given to us. The pattern of our life has been dictated by two core ideas. We strive to be faithful to the opportunities God sends our way. And we try to give ourselves to those opportunities completely.

I firmly believe life has a sense of order and direction to it. The order is simple—put God first. Once we are in the habit of putting God first the direction becomes simple as well. We make decisions that move us toward God.

Paul gave his spiritual son Timothy a strong reminder of how this can work. He established this challenge to Timothy on the precept of generosity. In giving of himself Timothy was to build a truly remarkable life.

I've seen these principles play out again and again in my own life. Living generously takes your life in a direction that sometimes seems confusing in the moment, but is hard to regret in the aftermath. If you dedicate yourself to giving your days over to the generous work of God, one day you will find yourself recounting memory after memory of many amazing things God has done around you.

FOR REFLECTION OR DISCUSSION:

Has it been a challenge for me to put God first in my life?

_____
_____
_____
_____
_____

If so, what have been the obstacles? If not, what outcomes have I seen resulting from that decision?

_____
_____
_____
_____
_____

CHALLENGE:

Share with someone in your small group or Sunday morning class what you believe to be your highest priorities and how having clarity about those priorities has helped you with direction and decision making.

Enjoy "Generational Generosity"?
Check out the following resources.

The Wisdom Trail Guide: 31 Steps to a Life of Wisdom

Paperback & eBook – July 2021
by Nathan King

"Wisdom is not something God wants *from* you. It's something God wants *for* you."

Wisdom is not something reserved for a select few. Wisdom is not meant to be hidden away from you. Wisdom is available to everyone. God wants you to experience a life of Wisdom. Nathan King has been helping others take their next step toward the life of Wisdom God wants for them for two decades.

"The Wisdom Trail Guide: 31 Steps to a Life of Wisdom" offers insight from 31 daily entrees in the Book of Proverbs. Each entry offers practical insight coupled with real life situations anyone searching for Wisdom can relate to.

"The Wisdom Trail Guide" is formatted to be a quick and easy read. One that doesn't consume a lot of your time; but offers a thoughtful response for each day. Read it on your own, with a friend, or in a group. The challenges and prayers included inside will help you take your next step forward.

In *"The Wisdom Trail Guide"* pastor and adjunct professor Nathan King lays out 31 clear steps anyone can take. Steps that can reshape how you see yourself, how you interact with the people around you, and how you approach your life.

Fear, forgiveness, decision making, friends, work, family and more are tackled during the four week journey that will challenge and encourage the life of anyone looking to take their next step toward a life of Wisdom.

Learn Love Live:
The Story God Wants for Your Life

Paperback & eBook – January 2022
by Nathan King

What if YOU could live a better story?

You have a story. It is the story of the life you are living, the ones you love, and the way God is helping you learn to follow Him. Your story is incredible, because it is yours. I know this because I have lived it. Living through each of these things has taught me the power of the love God has for us. It has shown me just how amazing life becomes when we begin to love the people around us in amazing ways. The way God wants us to. So, what does God want for you? Easy. He wants you to ...

LEARN. LOVE. LIVE.
The Story God Wants for Your Life

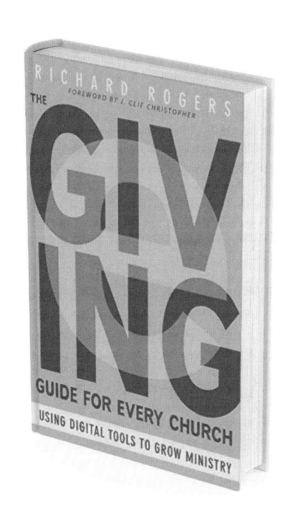

The E-Giving Guide for Every Church: Using Digital Tools to Grow Ministry

Paperback – October 2016
by Richard Rogers (Author), J. Clif Christopher (Foreword)

The purpose of this book is to help churches raise more money for ministry and mission by better using electronic media.

Although philanthropy in the US is growing, churches continue to receive a declining portion of that philanthropy. Part of the challenge is that America is becoming significantly less dependent on paper currency (cash and checks) yet many churches continues to count on paper currency as a primary media for donations. There have been warning signals for several years. Many churches face shrinking budgets and membership and are beginning to ask the right questions. The author's goal is to capture this teachable moment with a resource that will encourage pastors and church leaders to utilize tools already available to change the trajectory of their resourcing; because nothing is more important than what God has called them to do.

The banking and electronic giving industries have not made it easy for churches to understand their services or fees. This book will provide basic strategies and take the confusion and fear away, opening churches to new possibilities.

Dare to Parent: Dangerous Roads Ahead

Paperback – January 2020
By Jennifer Rogers

You will be encouraged with this mom's challenge to continue the fight for your family. If you're not being intentional with your parenting you are losing the battle for your kids. The world is telling your children who they are and who they should be, don't just let them out there to make these hard decisions on their own. Dare to Parent will give you seven anchors you can establish for your children to grow up to be responsible, enjoyable adults with the opportunity to do anything. It's the author's intent to share from her heart and tell you, "Stand Strong. It's not going to be the easy way but it's worth it to parent hard." Jennifer Rogers is a mom of 6. For 28 years she and her husband, Richard, have been intentionally parenting and they believe the family is the most powerful team in the world.

Nathan King lives with his family in Arkansas. You can often find him riding his bike off the side of a mountain, building something with his hands, or catching the latest superhero movie with his family. He also serves as an adjunct professor at his alma mater Arkansas Tech University. He and Jamie have the distinct privilege of serving as pastors at New Life Church in Conway, AR. You can find him online at www.nathanking.com or in his neighborhood walking his dog. For speaking inquiries contact help@nathanking.com.

Richard Rogers serves as a Ministry Strategist with Horizons Stewardship. In his early career, Richard worked as a manager for a Fortune 500 company developing young managers into leaders and encouraging them to pursue their potential. Now, with over 20 years of experience working with pastors and church leaders, Richard's aspiration is raising levels of discipleship, particularly in the area of generosity, to enable God's vision to become a reality. Throughout Richard's tenure in the local church, his leadership and focus on faith development helped his congregation experience a 70% increase in giving.

During his ministry with Horizons, he has partnered with churches across a variety of denominations and geographic regions in successful capital campaigns raising from over $13 million dollars to just over $300 thousand dollars. In recent years he has continuously worked with clients in annual campaigns and coaching agreements to increase regular giving and strengthen their culture of stewardship, giving, and generosity. His Next Level Generosity coaching references include numerous churches, an Episcopal Diocese, and the Superintendent of a K-12 private Christian school. Richard is a member of the International Coaching Federation.

Richard loves to have lunch and dinner dates with his wife, Jennifer. They are new grandparents and enjoy traveling to new places.

Made in the USA
Columbia, SC
10 January 2025

51538805R00059